BASKETBALL LEGENDS

Kareem Abdul-Jabbar
Charles Barkley
Larry Bird
Wilt Chamberlain
Clyde Drexler
Julius Erving
Patrick Ewing
Anfernee Hardaway
The Head Coaches
Grant Hill
Juwan Howard
Allen Iverson
Magic Johnson
Michael Jordan
Shawn Kemp
Jason Kidd
Reggie Miller
Alonzo Mourning
Hakeem Olajuwon
Shaquille O'Neal
Gary Payton
Scottie Pippen
David Robinson
Dennis Rodman
John Stockton

CHELSEA HOUSE PUBLISHERS

BASKETBALL LEGENDS

SHAWN KEMP

Mike Bonner

CHELSEA HOUSE PUBLISHERS
Philadelphia

Produced by The Type Shoppe Inc.
Chestertown, Maryland

Picture research by Lydia Wagner
Cover illustration by Bradford Brown

First Printing

1 3 5 7 9 8 6 4 2

Library of Congress Cataloging-in-Publication Data

Bonner, Mike, 1951–
        Shawn Kemp/Mike Bonner.
                p. cm. — (Basketball Legends)
        Includes bibliographical references (p.) and index.
        Summary: Describes the basketball career and personal life of the NBA
power forward from Elkhart, Indiana.
        ISBN 0-7910-4576-5 (hc)
        1. Kemp, Shawn, 1969- —Juvenile literature. 2. Basketball players—
United States—Biography—Juvenile literature. 3. Seattle Supersonics
(Basketball team)—Juvenile literature. [1. Kemp, Shawn, 1969- . 2. Basket–
ball players. 3. Afro-Americans—Biography.]
        I. Title. II. Series.
        GV884.K45B66   1998
                                                    97-43799
                                                        CIP
                                                        AC

CONTENTS

BECOMING A BASKETBALL LEGEND

Chuck Daly

What does it take to be a basketball superstar? Two of the three things it takes are easy to spot. Any great athlete must have excellent skills and tremendous dedication. The third quality needed is much harder to define, or even put in words. Others call it leadership or desire to win, but I'm not sure that explains it fully. This third quality relates to the athlete's thinking process, a certain mentality and work ethic. One can coach athletic skills, and while few superstars need outside influence to help keep them dedicated, it is possible for a coach to offer some well-timed words in order to keep that athlete fully motivated. But a coach can do no more than appeal to a player's will to win; how much that player is then capable of ensuring victory is up to his own internal workings.

In recent times, we have been fortunate to have seen some of the best to play the game. Larry Bird, Magic Johnson, and Michael Jordan had all three components of superstardom in full measure. They brought their teams to numerous championships, and made the players around them better. (They also made their coaches look smart.)

I myself coached a player who belongs in that class, Isiah Thomas, who helped lead the Detroit Pistons to consecutive NBA crowns. Isiah is not tall—he's just over six feet—but he could do whatever he wanted with the ball. And what he wanted to do most was lead and win.

All the players I mentioned above and those whom this series will chronicle are tremendously gifted athletes, but for the most part, you can't play professional basketball at all unless you have excellent skills. And few players get to stay on their team unless they are willing to dedicate themselves to improving their talents even more, learning about their opponents, and finding a way to join with their teammates and win.

It's that third element that separates the good player from the superstar, the memorable players from the legends of the game. Superstars know when to take over the game. If the situation calls for a defensive stop, the superstars stand up and do it. If the situation calls for a key pass, they make it. And if the situation calls for a big shot, they want the ball. They don't want the ball simply because of their own glory or ego. Instead they know—and their teammates know—that they are the ones who can deliver, regardless of the pressure.

The words "legend" and "superstar" are often tossed around without real meaning. Taking a hard look at some of those who truly can be classified as "legends" can provide insight into the things that brought them to that level. All of them developed their legacy over numerous seasons of play, even if certain games will always stand out in the memories of those who saw them. Those games typically featured amazing feats of all-around play. No matter how great the fans thought the superstars were, these players were capable of surprising the fans, their opponents, and occasionally even themselves. The desire to win took over, and with their dedication and athletic skills already in place, they were capable of the most astonishing achievements.

CHUCK DALY, now the head coach of the Orlando Magic, guided the Detroit Pistons to two straight NBA championships in 1989 and 1990. He earned a gold medal as coach of the 1992 U.S. Olympic basketball team—the so-called "Dream Team"—and was inducted into the Pro Basketball Hall of Fame in 1994.

HIS BEST GAME EVER

Shawn Kemp's forehead glistened with sweat as he approached the free throw line. Throughout the critical 1996 National Basketball Association Western Conference Finals, the Seattle SuperSonics' power forward had battled underneath the basket with the great Utah Jazz forward Karl "The Mailman" Malone.

On this day, June 2, 1996, in the last game of a seven-game series, a coveted NBA championship berth was on the line. Despite the Sonics' talent and superb 64–18 regular season record, fans in Seattle's KeyArena were nervous. They knew the Utah Jazz deserved a lot of credit for taking this final game down to the wire.

But Kemp had everything he needed to play basketball at the NBA level. He was 6'10", had a sturdy 260-pound frame, and possessed the physical skills necessary. He could shoot, dunk, defend, and crash the boards with the best of the big men.

Shawn Kemp takes a break during an NBA game in Seattle against Miami.

Karl Malone of the Utah Jazz closely guards Shawn Kemp in Game 7 of the 1996 Western Conference Finals.

"To win this last game," Seattle coach George Karl said, "we need to get big plays from Shawn underneath the basket."

Kemp felt the pressure as much as anybody. "I haven't won a championship game since junior high," Kemp said, the day before the final game. "I'm eager to play."

But there were experts who complained that something was missing from Kemp's game. He sometimes showed immaturity, they said. At other times he was inconsistent. When it counted, he didn't make the big plays.

After four quarters of superhuman struggle, Kemp's battle with "The Mailman" was nearly a draw. Then, with just 13.9 seconds left in the contest, Utah's Greg Foster fouled Kemp.

Holding the basketball in his huge hands, Kemp stared down at the high gloss floor of brand new KeyArena in Seattle. He gave himself a quiet pep talk before he took aim. Kemp bounced the ball on the floor several times. He glanced up at the basket.

It was easy to guess why the Jazz had picked on Kemp for the foul. The Sonics led the Jazz by only a single point, 87–86. Kemp had to make both shots to stretch the Sonics' lead to three. As a good but not spectacular free throw shooter, Kemp went to the line with a season average of 74 percent. Never was a pair of free throws more important to a player or his team. Making these foul shots took on added importance because the Sonics had choked miserably the previous two seasons, losing both times in the first playoff round.

As he stood at the line, Kemp had to be thinking about 1994, when he blew two foul shots that would have eliminated the Denver Nuggets from the playoffs. Because of those misses, Denver went on to beat the favored Sonics in overtime and took them out of the 1994 playoffs. A year later, in 1995, the Denver nightmare repeated itself, this time by the underdog Los Angeles Lakers.

Given his history, sinking a shot in a clutch situation like the one he faced now was no sure thing for Kemp. The 17,000 fans in the sold-out arena held their breath as Kemp let the ball fly to the hoop.

Would the shot go in? The silent Seattle fans froze as the ball floated toward the hoop. They had seen their beloved Sonics in this spot too many times before.

In truth, most Seattle fans felt that the game probably shouldn't have come down to this last, heart-stopping shot. They figured the Sonics would have swept the Jazz just as they had swept the feared Houston Rockets in only four games during the month of May. But the feisty Jazz had spoiled the party. After losing the first two games of the series to the Sonics, the Utah Jazz responded with a gutty 96–76 win in the third game. Then, in the fourth game, the Sonics edged the Jazz by two points, winning 88–86. With three games left, the series stood at 3–1 in favor of the Sonics. All the men from Seattle had to do was win one more victory to put them in the NBA Finals! But Utah won the next two games, including a demoralizing 118–83 blowout in Salt Lake City. The lopsided defeat clearly spelled trouble for the Sonics, reminding them of their quick exits from the playoffs in 1994 and 1995.

By Sunday, June 2, 1996, the chips were down for the Seattle SuperSonics. One advantage was that this last game was being played on their home court in Seattle. But, if the Sonics were going to make it to the NBA Finals against Michael Jordan's Chicago Bulls, Shawn Kemp would have to step up and play his best game ever.

From the start, the Sonics were tight and more than a little tense. The Jazz built a 15–7 lead in the first period. After a Kemp dunk finally ripped through the hoop, the Sonics relaxed and went on a 13–2 scoring run. Karl Malone added four points for the Jazz to close first-quarter scoring, which ended in a 21-point tie.

Before the game, Seattle coach George Karl had told his players to get the ball in low to Kemp, where his great strength and agility would pay off for the Sonics. In the second period, neither team got much leverage and the lead never grew larger than three points. At halftime, the Sonics led by a slim 44–41 margin. But as usual, the Jazz wouldn't quit, and in the first half, every shot the Sonics put up faced a suffocating Utah defense.

Under the boards, Kemp fought Malone, Hornacek, Stockton, and rising star Russell for every shot, loose ball, and rebound. Although his individual play shone, he couldn't do it alone. He relied on teammates Sam Perkins, Gary Payton, Detlef Schrempf, and Hersey Hawkins to come through. Kemp's comrades responded well, each scoring in double figures.

As the buzzer sounded to start the second half, the Sonics and Jazz went at each other with an intensity that hardly seemed human. In the dizzy array of flying feet, raised arms, and squeaking shoes, Shawn Kemp was everywhere at once. Midway through the third quarter, he took a pass, turned, and jammed the ball through the hoop with a resounding dunk. A few minutes later, Hersey Hawkins swiped the ball from Malone and zinged it to Kemp on a cross-court pass. WHAM! Kemp, the red-hot Sonic in the crisp home whites, slammed through another beautiful dunk.

Down but not out, the Jazz clawed back, keeping the game close as the fourth quarter neared. Utah Jazz coach Jerry Sloan called a time-out, alarmed because Kemp, Payton, and Hawkins were busting through Utah's packed screens to reach the basket. By the end of the third period, the Seattle lead had grown to six, 73–67. The Sonics benefited by shooting a blistering 61 percent, but Utah wouldn't give up and the stage was set for Kemp's stunning fourth period dramatics.

Sonics forward Shawn Kemp leaps up in jubilation as Seattle wins the Western Conference Finals in Seattle.

During the final period the game seesawed as it had done earlier. The Sonics suddenly went cold from the field, putting up 13 shots but only making 4 of them, rattled by a furious Utah defense. Equally poor shooting by the Jazz, however, kept Seattle in the lead. The Sonics' switching, trapping defense bullied the usually smooth Jazz offense, and they repeatedly missed critical free throws that would have put them ahead. Malone in particular couldn't seem to connect, enduring one of the worst free throw outings in his long career.

As the final minute approached, Seattle coach George Karl again directed his troops to pound the ball inside to Kemp. That's exactly what they were doing when Kemp was fouled with 13.9 seconds showing on the clock. The score was a razor thin 87–86 in favor of the Sonics. Now Shawn Kemp was facing the biggest test in the biggest game of his career. He shot, following through in a huge motion as the critical free throw left his hands.

It went in! KeyArena exploded in cheers.

Kemp's second foul shot also sailed through the rim. There would be no repeat of the Denver nightmare. The hometown fans roared their approval. In the last seconds of the game, Kemp had given Seattle a three-point lead! But the game wasn't over yet.

The Jazz quickly took a time-out and coach Sloan called a pick and roll play, the kind of play veteran stars like Malone and Stockton can run in their sleep. Stockton took the ball and faked as if he was going for a three pointer. As soon as the Seattle defenders rushed to him, he zipped the ball to Karl Malone. Kemp could not prevent Malone from reaching the basket. He had no choice but to foul him with a block to the body. Although Malone was expecting the hit, he missed the easy layup. Again, a likely three-point play came down to a pair of free throws. The game clock showed 8.2 seconds left.

Malone had been shooting free throws poorly throughout the series. With one last chance to deliver, he disappointed his team. He missed both attempts and gave the Sonics the win. The Sonics would meet Chicago in the NBA Finals!

Kemp's numbers in the seventh Western Conference game were impressive. He collected 26 points, 14 rebounds, and made 10 of 11 free throws. After the game, family and friends crowded around the victorious Sonics and a happy but drained George Karl.

Basketball fans who watched Kemp and the Sonics defeat a physical Utah squad saw something besides an exciting game. They saw Shawn Kemp emerge as not only the strength of his team, but also its heart. Kemp's renewed confidence and maturity would influence everything the Sonics did from now on. The Sonics were the Western Conference champions because Shawn Kemp had played his best game ever.

Shawn and his teammates celebrate their win over the Utah Jazz.

2

THE KID FROM ELKHART

Elkhart, Indiana, is a small industrial city populated by about 45,000 people. The city is in the far northern part of the state, where it nearly touches the Michigan border.

When they aren't at work, the residents of Elkhart, like most folks in Indiana, can be found attending basketball games or watching them at home on television. They are crazy about basketball!

Shawn Travis Kemp was born in Elkhart on November 26, 1969. His sister, Lisa, also an athlete, was a major influence on her brother as they were growing up, constantly challenging him in sports, especially basketball. His mother, Barbara, worked in the medical records department of a hospital to support her son and daughter. Around town, the Kemps were known as a close and loving family and Barbara Kemp as a woman of high personal standards.

Shawn Kemp raises his arm in a victory sign as Seattle fans roar their approval at Game 4 of the NBA Final in Seattle, June 12, 1996.

17

Kemp's intelligence and sensitivity flourished in the warm family environment provided by his mother and sister. So, too, did his basketball skills. "Lisa was competitive with me," Shawn said later. "She's the one that really got me interested in basketball."

In Elkhart, Shawn and his friends hung out together and played sports. Indoors during the winter and outdoors anytime the weather allowed, the kids played basketball. At first he was not good at basketball or any other sport. He had to wear braces on his legs and ankles because he had grown so fast his bones could not properly support his weight.

Shawn attended Eastside Elementary School. Once the braces came off, he was ready to play basketball for the school team and within two years, he was the best player Eastside had ever seen. The basketball-crazy folks in Indiana saw right from the start that he had major talent.

Although Shawn was not a good student, his mother went out of her way to keep her son focused on school and sports, in that order. Barbara Kemp felt sports would shield her son from the many dangers young people face on the streets, and Shawn knew he wanted to avoid drugs and petty crime. "Growing up, my dream was to go to college, have fun, and maybe someday get a chance to play in the NBA. I was sure I could make my dream happen if I worked hard and gave 100 percent."

After grade school, Kemp went on to Concord Junior High. Almost immediately he showed the talent and determination it takes to become a star player. By the time he was ready to play for the Concord High Minutemen, he was a local legend in Elkhart and his high flying acrobatics on the court were the talk of the town.

Kemp's high school coach Jim Hahn praised his athletic ability, which was sensational for a high school player. Hahn remembered that Kemp's dunks were downright spectacular. "I can recall several times when I'm about ready to jump out of my skin because one of the guards is throwing a pass out of the gym. And then suddenly this hand comes from out of nowhere and puts it through the rim. Afterwards I'm thinking, yeah, that was a good pass, on account of Shawn."

Everyone knew who the star player was. Kemp averaged 19.8 points per game, 12.9 rebounds, and 4 blocks. As early as his sophomore year, basketball fans started asking for his autograph. By the time he reached his senior year, he stood 6'10" and weighed over 200 pounds. Often, pro caliber players grow during their college years, building muscle and putting on weight, but Shawn already had a body big enough for the NBA.

College recruiters like Kentucky's Dwane Casey gushed over Kemp's efforts in practice and at games. "Bar none, Shawn Kemp was the finest player ever to come out of the state of Indiana. He showed he could play like nobody else."

Many college scouts were after Kemp. One who got on board early was Tim Grgurich, then assistant coach at the University of Nevada, Las Vegas. Grgurich started following Kemp when he was only 14, hoping that he might decide to play for the UNLV Runnin' Rebels. Later, Kemp and Grgurich were re-

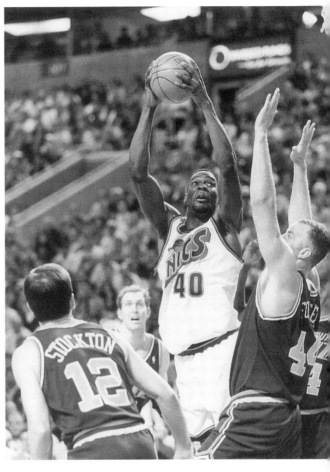

Shawn Kemp shoots around the outstretched arms of Jazz center Greg Foster.

united when Grgurich was hired as a Sonics assistant coach.

Meanwhile, Kemp spent long hours in the gym learning the game of basketball and constantly working to refine his skills.

At a basketball All Star game, Shawn met Chris Mills, a friend whose influence was to shape his life. Both Shawn and Chris saw themselves as future NBA players and became close friends.

When Kemp took the Scholastic Aptitude Test in preparation for going to college, he did poorly. Failure to get a good score meant that he would have to attend college as a Proposition 48 student. All Proposition 48 collegiate athletes had to wait out their freshman year and concentrate on academics. Proposition 48 came to be because the National Collegiate Athletic Association believed too many young athletes were not getting an education. The NCAA fostered Proposition 48 to ensure that colleges would at least try to educate their athletes.

When it came time to choose a college, Kemp announced that he would attend the University of Kentucky, where his friend Chris Mills was going. Many fans in Indiana took his decision to play out of state as an insult. Rude and badly behaved fans from rival high schools took to badgering Kemp with catcalls and ape-like noises. Exceptionally cruel fans once threw bananas at him. When opposing fans began chanting "SAT! SAT! SAT!" to rattle and embarrass him, Concord High fans would shout back "NBA! NBA! NBA!"

Kemp must have been hurt by the vicious taunting he endured but he did not let it show. He never let fans interfere with his determination to play top-notch basketball. And nothing altered his decision to attend the University of Kentucky.

At the University of Kentucky, Shawn found little to occupy his time. As a Proposition 48 student, he sat out his first semester as a college basketball player. Because he had never been much of a student, going without basketball was particularly tough on him. "It was difficult to have basketball taken away from me," Kemp said. "I went through a hard time."

Kemp couldn't have picked a worse time to attend Kentucky. In the fall of 1988, there were rumors that Coach Eddie Sutton's basketball program was soon to be the subject of a full NCAA investigation.

His original reason for choosing Kentucky had much to do with his friendship with Chris Mills. But soon after they became teammates at the college, a strange incident occurred. A package containing $1,000 in cash came open in transit. The sender was the University of Kentucky Athletic Department. The person to whom it was addressed was Chris Mills.

A scandal ensued. College basketball players cannot receive money for participating in sports beyond an athletic scholarship, and sending secret payments to players is a serious violation of NCAA rules. As a result of the incident, Eddie Sutton, assistant coach Dwane Casey, and the entire Kentucky basketball program were charged with 17 different recruiting infractions.

Some of the trouble spread to Shawn Kemp. Police officers in Lexington questioned him about a pair of gold necklaces that had been stolen from coach Eddie Sutton's son, Sean. Although Kemp denied that he had taken the jewelry, the damage was done and he left the University of Kentucky under a cloud.

Shortly after Thanksgiving 1988, assistant coach Dwane Casey phoned Red Spencer, a community college coach in Texas. Casey and Spencer arranged a deal that would allow Kemp to attend Trinity Valley Community College on a team manager's scholarship. Spencer had a long-standing reputation in college circles as a man who could take academically challenged and troubled players in hand. In return for playing for Spencer's TVCC squad, the player got another crack at college.

Kemp was perfect for the program. He arrived at Trinity Valley in the first week of December and immediately went to see his new coach. Spencer explained how the program worked and what would be expected of him. "I suppose I've let a lot of people down," Kemp said. "Never mind that," Spencer told him. "If you conduct yourself properly here, everything will work out fine."

At TVCC, Kemp practiced with the rest of the Cardinals although he still could not compete in a regular game. The other players and coaches were impressed with him, and Red Spencer was sure that Kemp would help his team win games.

He roomed with Don Reynolds, a player who had flunked out of the University of Texas. "Shawn Kemp was just like he is now," Reynolds said. "He was thinking about what to do—either continue in school or go into the NBA." Making it in the National Basketball Association was tough for anybody, but going straight from high school to the world's top professional league was considered almost impossible. Only a few had ever done it. The most famous was Moses Malone, who in the 1970s quit college to join the Utah Stars, a club in the American Basketball Association.

Could Shawn duplicate Malone's feat? The thought was much on his mind as he practiced with the Cardinals. He considered his options but kept mum on the subject while continuing to dazzle everyone with his incredible strength and quickness. "He dunked the ball so hard I once saw him take down an outdoor rim," said Don Reynolds. "He hung it in our room."

Coach Spencer could not have been happier with him. Kemp went to practice without fail and attended all his classes. The coach began to dream about all the games the Cardinals would win with Kemp at forward, but Shawn had other ideas.

One day in the early spring of 1989, Kemp told Spencer he had decided to enter the NBA draft. "I've been talking to some professional teams," Kemp said. "They all tell me I'll be a first round NBA pick."

Although he was disappointed, Spencer could see why Kemp wanted to go professional. "I didn't feel any ill will about his decision to turn pro," Spencer said. "I was just a little sorry for myself."

At the age of 19 and without any college experience, Kemp declared himself for the 1989 NBA draft. He worked out privately for a handful of NBA teams in preparation for draft day, including the Detroit Pistons and the Seattle SuperSonics.

On June 3, 1989, Seattle selected Shawn Kemp as the 17th pick in the first round. After a brilliant high school career and an abortive college career, Shawn Kemp was headed for the pros!

3

ON TO
SEATTLE

Seattle fans who gathered to watch the 1989 NBA draft on television loudly booed the choice of Shawn Kemp. Few had ever heard of him and many believed the Sonics had made a poor selection.

Seattle Times sports columnist Blaine Newnham echoed these sentiments when he told his readers not to be distracted by the choice of Kemp in the draft. "The really important people in this draft are Dana Barros and Brad Sellers," he wrote.

The Sonics picked two players in the first round, taking Boston College guard Dana Barros before Kemp as pick number 16. Although the 5'11" Barros was a popular player for the Sonics for four years, he was never a starter and often played poorly on defense. The other Seattle pick, 7'0" Brad Sellers, lasted less than a year with the Sonics and played in a total of only 45 games.

Shawn Kemp slam-dunks the ball in a game against the Denver Nuggets.

Sixteen other players were chosen before Kemp. Hardly any of them remain in the NBA, and none turned out to be as superior an NBA player in the long run as the young forward just barely out of high school.

The brains behind the Sonics' choice of Kemp was Seattle general manager Bob Whitsitt. After watching Kemp in a private workout, both Whitsitt and coach Bernie Bickerstaff were astounded. "Here's a 6'10", 240-pound kid handling the ball on the break, swishing three pointers like they're layups and dominating everybody inside," Bob Whitsitt said. "How could we not take him?"

Kemp arrived in Seattle with little more than hope and a dream. In September 1989 the club signed Kemp to a contract that seemed pretty rich for a college dropout but was cheap by NBA standards. The deal, a virtual steal, was a six-year pact that saw Kemp making $650,000 by his fourth season. If he did not make the club, he wouldn't get paid anything.

Kemp joined a successful Seattle team that had gone 47–35 the previous season. Sonics coach Bernie Bickerstaff plugged Kemp into a top quality lineup. Besides the rookies, the squad included veterans Dale Ellis, Xavier McDaniel, Derrick McKey, Nate McMillan, Sedale Threatt, and Michael Cage.

Even though he was still an underage rookie player, Kemp won the respect of his teammates with his ability to learn and his intense desire to play the game. In Kemp's first year, the Sonics relied on Ellis, McDaniel, and McKey to shoulder the scoring burden. Kemp played a secondary role, concentrating on rebounding and learning the NBA game. He was a quick study. "At first you'd be able to make a move on Shawn," said teammate Michael Cage. "But the next time around he'd be doing that same move on you, only better."

Coach Bickerstaff brought Kemp off the bench in 81 games his first season, playing him for longer stretches as the season wore on. While the Sonics were successful at home, compiling a 30–11 record, they were exactly the opposite on the road, 11–30. With only limited playing time, Kemp averaged 6.5 points per game and 4 rebounds. But he was off to a good start and fans who had initially ignored him began to warm up.

Forceful and stylish dunks soon became a hallmark of his on-court play. After slamming the ball through, Kemp would often celebrate as he rushed back on defense. His display of emotion invariably got the crowd into the game.

Kemp entered the slam dunk competition at the All Star game in his rookie year and for several years thereafter. He never won, although he did come in second during the 1991 All Star weekend.

As his playing time increased, Kemp learned a lot from fellow forward Xavier McDaniel, known as "X Man." A six-year veteran from Wichita State, McDaniel quickly spotted Kemp as a great talent. The two forwards spent hours together and formed a fast friendship. "Shawn would ask me about things," McDaniel said, "and I would tell him what he had to do to survive in this league."

The Houston Rockets' Clyde Drexler gets a steal from Shawn Kemp.

"The way I saw the Sonics going," Kemp said, "was that X Man was going to be the small forward and I was going to be power forward. But that's not how it turned out."

During the 1988-89 season, the Sonics finished third in the Pacific Division, ten games behind the Lakers. In the playoffs, the Sonics needed four games to beat the Houston Rockets in the first round. Then they suffered a four-game sweep by the Lakers in the Western Conference Semifinals. The Lakers were themselves swept in four games by the Chuck Daly-coached Detroit Pistons that year.

Kemp's success eventually made McDaniel expendable to the Sonics. Seattle traded the savvy, soft-spoken McDaniel to Phoenix early in Kemp's second season. A gracious man of remarkable personal warmth, McDaniel broke the news to Kemp himself. "I told Shawn that this was his team now, and this was his chance to make something of it."

"I couldn't believe it when they traded X Man," Kemp said. "I was very sorry to see him go."

People who know Shawn are aware of the enormous loyalty he has to his teammates. His comrades on the court are also loyal to him. They know how much he gives of himself to the game and how much playing basketball at the professional level means to him personally.

In his first two years, ball handing sometimes proved to be a problem for Kemp. The players he faced when playing for Concord High in Elkhart were pushovers compared to the players he faced in the NBA. In his rookie year, he committed 107 turnovers, a lot for a guy who was only on the court about 13 minutes a game.

On the personal front, Kemp slowly adjusted to life in Seattle. His mother went to Seattle to help him set up housekeeping. Once she had things in order, she left him alone. "She said the experiences I needed to go through, I needed to go through on my own," Kemp said. "She was right."

The next year big changes were in order for the .500 Sonics, who in 1989–90 had missed the playoffs for the first time in five seasons. Gone from the team was shooter Dale Ellis, traded to the Milwaukee Bucks. Also gone was fellow rookie Brad Sellers, the player many fans and sportswriters thought would be better than Kemp.

In the 1990 draft, the Sonics plucked race-horse guard Gary Payton from Oregon State. Although Payton's perimeter game was considered suspect, he was a tiger on defense and had experience in running an offense.

More moves made by the front office included the acquisition of shooter Ricky Pierce for Ellis and the trade of Olden Polynice to the Clippers for Benoit Benjamin. They also brought in K. C. Jones, a former Boston Celtic, to coach the team. "I like this club," Jones said. "I believe we have the right mix of players, the right attitude. We're going to be an exciting team and I expect us to do well this year."

As with many personnel shuffles made by sports managers to upgrade a team, these deals ultimately had little effect on the fortunes of the Sonics. Players on winning teams often use the word "chemistry" to explain why they win. It refers to a quality within the hearts of the players, of their regard for each other, and of their desire to win. But the businessmen who control professional sports often pay little heed to the confidence players must have in each other in order to function effectively during a game.

Shawn Kemp did all he could as a second-year player to win the confidence of his teammates. He worked hard in practice, learning all the tricks, moves, and habits that help a player become an NBA superstar. But as a team, the Sonics did not play basketball as well as coach K. C. Jones expected.

Shawn Kemp's performance, however, improved enormously during the 1990–91 season. In the opening game, a 118–106 victory over the Houston Rockets, he pulled down 10 rebounds. In the second game he got 13 rebounds. K. C. Jones quickly found reasons to keep Kemp on the floor, playing him in 81 games and more than doubling his minutes on the court.

High-stepping Shawn Kemp is blocked in a game against the Nets at the Meadowlands Arena in New Jersey.

During a game against the Lakers on January 18, 1991, Kemp blocked 10 shots, an all-time Sonics record. At one point in the Lakers game, Laker Byron Scott put up what looked like an easy jumper, shooting from just outside the paint. Suddenly, from out of nowhere, Kemp's hand caught the ball and swatted it neatly into the arms of Gary Payton. A perfect block! The stunned Lakers scrambled to get back on defense. Payton raced downcourt to score on a layup, high-fiving Kemp as the Lakers inbounded. The Lakers won the game by a score of 105–96, but the Hollywood celebrities at courtside left the Los Angeles Forum marvelling about the second-year Sonic from Elkhart.

The 1990–91 Sonics went 41–41, losing games they should have won and pulling no

A reflective Shawn Kemp talks to reporters during the 1996 NBA Finals.

upsets. In the first round of the playoffs, the Sonics were beaten in five games by the Portland Trailblazers. For his part, Kemp improved his points-per-game average to 15.0, an astonishing increase, and every part of his game showed a dramatic improvement. Sonics watchers began to take particular note of the young forward who was strong and quick and played with incredible emotion.

Although Kemp improved, gossip around the NBA had it that the Sonics were talented but undermotivated. That was the reason for their 41–41 record. Something had to give.

The 1991–92 season began much like the previous season under K. C. Jones. Except for Kemp and a few others, the Sonics' overall play was not consistent. They'd be up for one game, down for the next. Sonics management decided to make a coaching change and hired George Karl, a former pro player. Karl had coached before in the NBA, the CBA, and in Europe, but his stints with two other NBA teams had run hot and cold. He was believed by many to be something of a smart aleck and he himself admitted it was sometimes true. But after failing in the NBA, he continued coaching and gained valuable experience at a lower professional level.

By 1992, Karl had learned his lesson and was itching for another chance in the big show. From the Sonics, the brash, brilliant coach got immediate results. In his first month as coach, February of 1992, he was named NBA coach of the month. The Sonics had gone 9–3.

Like the rest of the Sonics, Kemp responded to the new coach. Karl was different. He didn't seem to think having a huge center clogging up the middle was a good idea. He experimented with rotations. He loved defense. And he rarely called time-outs except when there was an emergency.

In the February 3 game at the Atlanta Hawks, Kemp collared 15 rebounds. On February 17, at home against the Phoenix Suns, Kemp was both leading scorer with 24 points and leading rebounder with 14. Better yet, against Phoenix, the Sonics won a close game against an excellent team in a 98–96 squeaker.

With Karl at the helm, the Sonics continued to win, finishing the year at 47–35. They also did reasonably well in the playoffs, beating Golden State in four games and losing to the Utah Jazz in five. Kemp was at his best in the playoffs, the moment that every professional basketball player lives for. In the series against Golden State, he averaged 22 points and 16.3 rebounds.

The fired-up Sonics eagerly awaited the 1992–93 season because they would finally get a chance to make a run at the championship.

Winning a championship is what every player dreams about. Although a few take comfort in personal statistics, the truth is that basketball is a team game. You win or lose with four other players. You're not out there alone. And it's impossible to win if all basketball means to you is simply a job. The best coaches know it; the best players know it; and the fans know it too.

Under Karl's coaching, the Sonics blossomed. He emphasized team play and self-sacrifice. As an NBA player, Karl had worked extra hard and had always been willing to take a charge on defense. He liked Shawn Kemp because he knew he put the team first. Shawn Kemp was a "George Karl" kind of player. With Karl at the helm, Kemp became a leader, not just in rebounding, but also in scoring and defense.

In the 1992–93 opener, Kemp ripped the Houston Rockets for 29 points and an incredible 20 rebounds. The Sonics gained momentum with every game, and Karl came to rely on Kemp more than ever. Kemp's fourth NBA season saw him mature into a whole performer, a player at the top of his game.

During the season, Kemp suffered a leg injury that caused him to miss 18 games, but he came back from the injury and was ready for the playoffs.

The team goal that year was to reach the NBA Finals, not just participate in the playoffs. Kemp led the way as the nearly unstoppable Sonics posted a 55–27 regular season mark, good for second place in the Pacific Division. The mark was just two games short of the 1979–80 Sonics' record, a team then coached by Lenny Wilkens. The club in 1979–80 had many legendary Sonics, including Jack Sikma, Fred Brown, Paul Silas, and Dennis Johnson.

Shawn Kemp flies after a loose ball with team-mate Gary Payton and Dallas Maverick Morlon Hilley (left) in close pursuit.

The Sonics of 1992–93 proved themselves every bit as good, beating Utah and Houston before being matched against Charles Barkley and the Phoenix Suns in the Western Conference Finals. The result was a tough, tight series. The Sonics fell to Phoenix in seven games, with Kemp the leading Seattle rebounder in every game except one. In Game 5, Kemp even poured in a series-high 33 points during a wild 120–114 loss to the Suns.

George Karl told his team not to be disappointed. He said he was proud of the way they had played and singled out Kemp's leadership for special praise. "We'll be back," Karl said. "That was just the beginning."

4

HIGHS AND LOWS

As the 1993–94 NBA season opened, the Sonics went on a tear the likes of which Seattle fans had never seen before. Still giddy from their near miss in reaching the NBA Finals in June, the Sonics came together to post a club record 63 wins. Shawn Kemp was no small part of their success.

The first regular season game took place at home on November 6, 1993. The Sonics blasted the always dangerous Los Angeles Lakers by a score of 129–101. Kemp led the way with a team high 30 points and 14 rebounds. On defense, the Sonics were super. Guard Gary Payton drew highly rated Laker rookie Nick Van Exel as his personal assignment. In the course of the game, Payton took the rookie to school, mercilessly defending him. Together, Kemp and Payton had no trouble making hash of the carefully drawn Laker plays.

Shawn Kemp and Gary Payton celebrate after a successful slam dunk.

Sonics Kendall Gill, Detlef Schrempf, and Sam Perkins also did a lot of damage to the L.A. Lakers. And when the perimeter was covered, they were more than happy to sling the ball to Kemp, who scored at will from inside the paint.

In the third period, the Sonics outscored the Lakers 35–19, including a dazzling fast break off a Van Exel turnover that ended in a thundering Kemp dunk.

Kemp's high-level performance set the tone for the first two months of the season. During that period, the Sonics only lost three games. The first loss came against Cleveland on November 27. Sonics coach George Karl blasted the refs. "They didn't want us to win," Karl said.

The next loss was a seven-point fall in a low-scoring 82–75 game against the Houston Rockets on December 11. The centerpiece of this hard-fought affair was a narrowly averted brawl.

Shawn Kemp drives past the Orlando Magic's Shaquille O'Neal in pursuit of the ball during a game in Seattle.

Even the losses were marked by Kemp's outstanding all-around play. He had 26 points and 14 rebounds in the loss to Cleveland. Against Houston, Kemp pulled down a team high of 12 rebounds.

A near disaster took place on December 14 when the Sonics hosted the Orlando Magic and their great young center, Shaquille O'Neal. In the second half, Kemp and O'Neal tangled as Kemp went up to shoot. On the way down, O'Neal got in Kemp's way, slamming him into a television camera and knocking him unconscious. O'Neal was ejected and Kemp suffered a bloody nose and a bruised left knee that forced him to miss three games.

Kemp hadn't fully recovered from his Orlando injury when the Sonics played the Phoenix Suns in Seattle before Christmas. The game resulted in one of those rare outings where Kemp was not high man in either points or rebounds. Nobody had to remind the Sonics that Phoenix had gone to the NBA Finals the year before instead of them. Although they were sky high for this regular season rematch, they lost when Phoenix guard/forward Dan Majerle swished a three pointer with seven seconds remaining to seal an 87–86 win.

In January, the Sonics endured a slump and lost five games. Another mini-slump occurred in March when they lost three games in an eight-day stretch. But each time the Sonics bounced back, with Kemp and company often playing some of their best basketball after a tough loss. A great motivator, Seattle coach George Karl rarely found fault with individual players, although he would often complain about the group as a whole.

During the 1993–94 season, there were only a few times when Karl had to chew out his players, and Kemp was almost never among the ones being reprimanded.

Even among the ultra-talented Sonics, Kemp was recognized as something special. Every year since he joined the league, he had learned ways to improve his shooting and fine-tune his moves to the rim. The 1993–94 season saw Kemp increase his points-per-game average to 18.1 and his total rebounds to 851. No longer was Kemp content to let the scoring be done by others. He worked hard to become the main man for the Sonics in all aspects of the game. He scored, rebounded, dished out assists, and defended. Asked to describe his work ethic, Kemp said: "I still have a long way to go, because I'm just scratching the surface. But I'm putting in the time and polishing things up and I think my game will keep improving until I stop working."

As the season rolled on the Sonics piled up more than three times as many wins as losses, finishing the year 63–19. Everyone from the front office to the hometown fans believed the team was sure to appear in the NBA Finals. Like the other Sonics, Kemp was eager for the challenge. "The NBA teams that are the most aggressive are the most successful," Kemp said. "We've had a great year because of our hard-nosed approach to the game."

The confident Sonics beat the Nuggets in the first two games, but all was not well with the team. At halftime in the second game, Gary Payton and Ricky Pierce shouted at each other. The tension was unbearable. In Game 3 the Sonics appeared sluggish and stayed that way. Playing not to lose instead of playing to win, they lost Games 3 and 4.

Shawn races toward the basket during a game against the Milwaukee Bucks in Tacoma, Washington.

In Game 5, fighting for their lives, the Sonics took the Nuggets into overtime. Denver grabbed its first lead of the extra period when Nuggets guard Reggie Williams swished a three pointer with 2:40 left. Kemp answered with a difficult basket over the towering Denver shot blocker Dikembe Mutombo, but it was the last two points the Sonics would score that season. Denver won the game 98–94, killing Seattle's hopes.

Nobody could believe it. The Sonics were out of the playoffs! Just like that! The world of professional basketball was shocked by the Sonics' early exit from post-season play. "They choked," said sportswriters, fans, and radio talk-show hosts. "The Sonics couldn't take the pressure."

Seattle coach George Karl took the loss just as hard as his team. "We're stunned," Karl said. "It's almost like having a death in the family." Kemp had little to say about the loss to Denver until the basketball season began again in the autumn of 1994.

In the summer of 1994, the Sonics' front office embarked on a peculiar deal, which would have sent Kemp to Chicago in return for Scottie Pippen. From an outsider's standpoint, such a trade appeared to offer the Sonics nothing. Worse, it appeared to hold distinct disadvantages. Despite the loss to Denver, Kemp was a key player in a smoothly functioning upper-level NBA team. The businessmen operating the individual franchises in the NBA, however, continually seek to gain advantages over one another, and the phrase "blockbuster trade" is never far from their lips. The Kemp-for-Pippen switch never materialized, but the damage to Kemp's outlook

Shawn answers reporters' questions after a team practice in Seattle.

was serious. "I think the trade talk bothered Shawn," said George Karl. "I think it would have bothered anyone."

But in spite of nearly being traded to Chicago, Kemp looked forward to the new season. "What happened to us last year makes you hungry," Kemp said. "It also makes you look forward to the playoffs. But there's a lot of games between now and then, so we have to be patient."

The 1994–95 Sonics' season began without the kind of success that marked the previous campaign. After the first seven games, the Sonics were 3–4. In late November, the team picked up the pace, putting together winning streaks of as many as ten games to finish out the season 57–25. It wasn't quite as good as the 63–19 record they had compiled in 1993–94, but it was good enough to qualify them for a high seed in the playoffs.

On the court, Kemp improved his performance once again, boosting his point total per game from 18.1 to 18.7. Rebounding also improved, with Kemp accounting for 893 grabs, both offensive and defensive. His rebound total was good enough to place him sixth in the league. Kemp's field goal percentage put him in the eighth spot among the 348 active NBA players.

A game full of highlights for Kemp took place on December 10, 1994. He scored 42 points against the Los Angeles Clippers at Anaheim. The Sonics needed the points to win, narrowly beating the Clippers 132–127 in overtime.

In short, it was an outstanding year for Shawn Kemp. Sportswriters and broadcasters covering the Sonics began to run out of words to describe his exceptional play, and around the league he earned the nickname "Reignman," which referred to his ability to rule the floor. Teammate Michael Cage had another theory concerning the name: "When Shawn's coming down on you, you can stop him about as much as you can stop the rain."

Along with team success came many personal accolades. Kemp was named an NBA All Star in 1993 and Second Team All NBA in 1994 and 1995. A spot on the U.S. gold medal-winning world championship team came Kemp's way in 1994, and he was named to the NBA All Star team in 1995 for the third season in a row.

This success was supposed to carry through to the playoffs, where the Sonics would redeem themselves for their first-round loss to Denver the year before. Although they did not finish first in the division, the Sonics finished only two games behind division-winner Phoenix.

In the first round, the Sonics drew the always-dangerous Los Angeles Lakers. The first game in the series resulted in a predictable 97–71

Seattle victory at the Tacoma Dome, home to the Sonics during the 1994–95 season while they waited for KeyArena to be completed. The second game saw the Lakers notch an 84–82 victory over the Sonics in the Dome, and the Sonics grew concerned. In each of the first two games, Kemp was the leader or co-leader in both scoring and rebounding, but the team as a whole seemed flat. Kemp collected 30 points in Game 3 and grabbed 11 rebounds, but it was not enough. The Lakers notched another slim 105–101 victory in Los Angeles. Meanwhile, worried fans, coaches, and players wondered aloud if the stage was being set for another playoff collapse by the snake-bitten Sonics. With their backs to the wall, the Sonics put everything they had on the line in the fourth game.

The first quarter sizzled as Lakers made seven of their first eight shots. However, the Sonics stole the ball from the Lakers half a dozen times, forging a 20–17 lead in the early going. By the end of the second period, the Sonics were up 59–55 and looking to extend their lead in the second half.

Kemp emerged from the first half with 8 rebounds and 14 points, just a single digit behind Gary Payton, who scored 15. In the second half, the Lakers used a three-guard rotation to neutralize the Sonics' defense. At first it didn't work, as Kemp and company worked furiously to stretch their lead 11 points to 76–65 midway through the third period. For a time, it looked like the Sonics would stay firmly in control. But Lakers guard Nick Van Exel pumped in eight points, six of them coming on a pair of three pointers, to put the Lakers right back in the game. It was

Shawn Kemp comes down screaming after slamming in two points in a game against the Golden State Warriors.

sweet revenge time for the Lakers guard, still smarting from countless past humiliations by the Sonics, especially Gary Payton.

As the fourth quarter opened, the Lakers went on an 11–3 run to tie the score at 96–96. By this time, the Los Angeles Forum crowd was in a frenzy for "Van Excellent." Everybody seemed to sense an upset in the making. But the Sonics hung on, holding a 108-107 lead with two minutes left to go in the game. Unfortunately, they missed all of their big shots from the line and allowed the Lakers to score their final seven points on free throws. As time expired, the scoreboard read Lakers 114, Sonics 110.

The Sonics had been bounced from the playoffs in the first round for the second straight year! Afterwards, Kemp could not bear to face reporters. Seattle coach George Karl told the media his team had not been strong enough mentally to win the playoff series. "We're a better team than we showed in the playoffs the last two years," Karl said. "Now it's time to face our embarrassment and be humbled, to feel the humility of sport. We'll try to figure something out and move on."

While his coach talked, Kemp remained in the visitors' locker room, his face in his hands. He was drained both physically and emotionally by his all-out effort in the loss.

The two emotions he felt most strongly were anger about what had happened, and pain for himself and his teammates.

Would Kemp be able to channel his emotions into greater exertions and greater success in the future? The upcoming 1995–96 season, his best ever, would supply the answer.

5

COMING THROUGH

James Naismith invented basketball in 1891 as a means of keeping his high-spirited YMCA gym class safely occupied during the long, cold New England winter. Much later, Naismith wrote a book about the game he had invented. In the book, he discussed the values he believed basketball taught those who pursue it as a serious activity. One of the values was emotional self-control. "A player who permits his feelings to interfere with his reflexes is a hindrance to his team."

Of the 12 values outlined by Naismith, self-control is the one that has troubled Shawn Kemp during his career. Perhaps his lack of self-control can be excused by his tender age or lack of college experience. But sometimes older and supposedly wiser players get out of control (Dennis Rodman, for example), while Moses Malone, who went straight to the NBA

Shawn Kemp passes the ball in front of Chicago Bulls center Luc Longley in Game 5 of the NBA Finals in Seattle on June 14, 1996.

from high school, always controls both his game and his temper.

Starting with the 1995–96 season, a more experienced, confident, and self-controlled Shawn Kemp appeared on the floor in his number 40 Sonics uniform. The Sonics opened the season with a 112–94 loss at the Utah Jazz on November 3. Although Kemp managed to snag eight rebounds, the leading scorer for the Sonics was the German-born Detlef Schrempf. But as the season wore on, wins quickly outpaced losses and it wasn't until January 10, 1996, that the Sonics' loss total reached two figures at 23–10.

The tenth loss came against the Chicago Bulls, who relied on the incomparable Michael Jordan to rip the Sonics 113–87. It was the biggest losing margin of the season up to that point. Kemp scored 17 points and pulled down 13 rebounds, trying desperately to compensate for a dismal Seattle effort. He could not pull it off.

After the game, Kemp said that they would have their hands full if they should happen to meet the Bulls in the NBA Finals later on. "Jordan is still a great player," Kemp said. "His game hasn't lost anything that I can see." Karl comforted his team by telling them there was still a lot of regular season basketball to go before the playoffs.

The 1995–96 season ended with a 64–18 record, the finest in club history and the tenth best mark in the history of the NBA. The Sonics entered the 1996 playoffs with a ferocious reputation on defense and led the league in steals for the fourth straight year. Both Kemp and Payton were named second team All NBA and Kemp was a starter in the All Star game.

The one sour note came on the last game of the season when Kemp was ejected for fighting with Tom Hammonds of the Nuggets. The ejection cost Kemp a chance to participate in the first playoff game against the Sacramento Kings. Once again, the issue of self-control troubled Kemp. The one-game suspension for fighting with Hammonds seemed to energize Kemp but unfortunately, not the Sonics. In Game 2, the Sacramento Kings beat Seattle by a score of 90–81. Keyed by the play of sharpshooting Kings guard Mitch Richmond, the Kings put forth their best effort. Even a team-leading 21 points and 8 rebounds by Kemp could not contain the inspired Kings. As it turned out, Game 2 was about all the fight the Kings had in them. Game 3 saw Seattle coast to a solid win. In Game 4, Kemp occupied the Kings inside, letting Payton run wild. The Seattle guard took advantage, putting down 29 points in a 101–87 victory that slammed the door on Sacramento. The first round jinx was over!

Shawn sports his Western Division Champion T-shirt after the Sonics' win over the Utah Jazz.

After Sacramento, the Houston Rockets presented less of a challenge to the surging Sonics. A four-game sweep of this top-rated team made the critics clam up. In the series, Kemp saved his best for last, exploding for 32 points and 15 rebounds in a 114–107 overtime thriller at The Summit in Houston.

The last obstacle to a coveted Finals berth was the Utah Jazz. Keyed by the powerhouse trio of Karl Malone, John Stockton, and Jeff Hornacek, the Jazz had already defeated both

Portland and San Antonio en route to a Western Conference Finals date with the Sonics.

It was well known that Shawn Kemp was an admirer of Karl Malone. Less well known was Malone's admiration for Kemp. "Kemp's definitely turned himself into a complete player," Malone said. "He seems to enjoy the game. It seems like he's having fun out there."

Shawn Kemp was having fun out there. Late in the second game of the Utah series, hosted by the Sonics in KeyArena, the Sonics led by only two points, 89–87, and the clock was running down. Less than half a minute remained in a tough, hard-fought, and foul-plagued contest. Kemp had spent half the game on the bench because of foul trouble. Late in the fourth period, George Karl sent him back in. He made two shots over Malone, the second of which gave Seattle the lead with 38 seconds left.

Utah came down the court, looking for a chance to tie the game. Stockton rocketed a pass across the court intended for Hornacek. Timing it perfectly, Kemp stepped in front of the pass. His steal preserved the win and the home fans went wild.

Seattle Times sports columnist Steve Kelley called the Kemp steal "a play that will echo in Sonic history for as long as the game is played in Seattle." Kemp was a little more modest. "You sit back there and you have a decision to make. If you gamble and lose, the game could be tied. But I thought I had a good feel on it. I felt like Gary Payton there for a minute."

In the series with Utah, the Sonics jumped out ahead, three games to one. Then, in two games marked by brilliant Utah play, the Jazz knotted the seven-game series 3–3. The pressure was on once again for the Sonics to come through in a clutch situation.

Fortunately for the Sonics, their superb performance in the regular season gave them the home court advantage for the last game. In a tough but ultimately successful battle, they won the right to meet Chicago for the 1996 NBA championship.

Shawn loses the ball to Nuggets center Ervin Johnson, but goes on to recover it.

The Seattle Supersonics played in their first NBA title game since the 1978–79 season when they met the Chicago Bulls on June 5, 1996, in Chicago. Few observers expected the Sonics to have a chance against the Bulls. Most sports fans outside of Seattle predicted a four-game Chicago sweep.

Seattle and Chicago followed the script in the first three games, with the Bulls outhustling, outshooting, and outplaying the Sonics at every turn. The Sonics weren't just overmatched; they were getting clobbered.

The first game ended with a solid Chicago win, 107–90, although Shawn Kemp's individual performance was practically flawless. He scored 32 points, many of them from the outside, where he was less likely to be double-teamed. But having to stray outside kept Kemp from grabbing his usual double-digit rebound total. Payton was the leading rebounder in Game 1 for the Sonics with 10.

NBA superstar Michael Jordan proved a particularly tough customer for the Sonics to handle. Although guard Gary Payton compared favorably to the stellar Jordan in terms of quickness, stealth, and ball-handling ability, Jordan's experience in the Finals often showed. And in the paint, where Kemp usually made his plays, Chicago forwards Toni Kukoc and Scottie Pippen came after him as if he was the only Sonic on the floor.

Chicago managed a narrow win in Game 2, a 92–88 squeaker that left Seattle fans heartsick with "what ifs" and "might have beens." Game 3 also went to the Bulls, a sound thrashing that put the Sonics on the brink of elimination. Undaunted, the Sonics regrouped and charged the Bulls in Games 4 and 5, with Shawn Kemp

Shawn Kemp hangs his head after the Sonics lose Game 3 of the NBA Finals to the Chicago Bulls.

and Gary Payton leading the way. Kemp's sterling 25-point, 11-rebound performance in Game 4 showed just how deep his Sonics pride ran. There would be no sweep. But on June 16, 1996, the Bulls dug into their bag of tricks and won 87–75 to take the championship.

After the Finals ended with a 4–2 Chicago triumph, Michael Jordan told reporters he considered Kemp the main man in the Sonics' arsenal. "I think he's the heart and soul of their team. I think a lot of people may call him man-child or immature or whatever, but this kid can play the game of basketball. I don't think the Sonics would be where they are without him."

As the 1996–97 season approached, Kemp became dissatisfied with his $3.7 million salary. He was miffed that despite his four-time All Star status, he was only the sixth highest paid player on the team. In stark contrast, teammate Gary Payton had an $88 million, seven-year contract. The Sonics knew they were underpaying Kemp but could do nothing about it. Under the rules, a player's contract could not be reworked until three years after it had been signed. Kemp stayed out of training camp for a time in October of 1996 to show that when his contract came up again in late 1997, he was going to bargain for keeps. This new attitude frustrated coach Karl and Sonics team president Wally Walker. Before he returned, Kemp issued a statement through his agent that he would be taking steps to make sure he got more money in the future. With NBA players like Shaquille O'Neal signing huge $120 million contracts, nobody was surprised that Shawn Kemp wanted his value demonstrated more clearly.

Kemp's value to his team can be measured in games where the Sonics are not necessarily playing their best ball. On January 8, 1997, the Sonics went to Denver to play the Nuggets in McNichols Arena. The night before, the Sonics had defeated the Miami Heat, one of the best teams in the East, at home in Seattle. Because the 1996–97 Sonics had not yet beaten any of the top three teams in the West—the Lakers, the Jazz, and the Houston Rockets—the win over the Atlantic Division-leading Heat was especially sweet.

As always after a big win, the temptation is to let down and simply "go through the motions." A letdown like the defeat the Sonics

*Shawn Kemp with
the ball in action
against Orlando
Magic defender
Horace Grant.*

suffered at the hands of Denver in the last game of the 1995–96 regular season was indeed possible. Near the end of the fourth period, it looked as if the Sonics might fall to the Nuggets. With less than three minutes to go, the Nuggets cut the lead to two points. Seattle answered with a basket to go up again by four. The Nuggets brought the ball up, seeking once again to cut Seattle's lead. The clock showed one minute 30 seconds remaining. The Nuggets got ready to run a play. Suddenly, moving like a cat, Kemp snatched the ball and raced downcourt, with Gary Payton trailing behind him. Kemp zipped the ball to Payton, who saw Sam Perkins cut open. Payton bounced the ball to Perkins, who scored an easy jumper. In one swift judo chop, Kemp had broken Denver. The game ended 109–99 in favor of the Sonics.

"You can't beat everybody big but tonight we got the job done," Kemp said. "Late in the game, you've got to have somebody doing the dirty work—that's me. In this league, you've got to bring it with you every night."

Gary Payton talked about how hard and how necessary it is to keep the team motivated. "Me and Shawn are the leaders of this team. I know I have to play hard every game because Shawn won't let down either. Winning like this helps us get our confidence up so we can beat the tough teams like Utah, Houston, and Chicago."

Ten days later in Cleveland, Kemp showed another side of his versatile game. In the third period, he crushed the Cavaliers with a pair of crucial three pointers. Kemp put the shots up over his old friend from grade school, Chris Mills. "Shawn's three at the end of the third quarter broke our momentum," Mills said. "You could see his confidence grow after that."

Despite slumping in the second half of the season, Kemp led the Sonics to the playoffs again, where they lost to the Houston Rockets in the Western Conference Semifinals. Then on September 25, 1997, the Sonics, aware of Kemp's frustration with his salary, dealt Kemp to the Cleveland Cavaliers in a three-team, five-player trade. The Cavs renegotiated his contract, and Kemp showed his gratitude by getting off to a quick start in 1997, leading his new team in both scoring and rebounding.

Kemp's newfound status as a major NBA star can be measured by the upward movement of Shawn Kemp sports memorabilia. Kemp is getting the national attention that makes his cards attractive to collectors. For example, Shawn Kemp basketball rookie cards have sharply risen in value since the appearance of the Sonics in the 1996 NBA Finals. In late 1995, Kemp's 1990–91 #279 NBA Hoops rookie card sold for only $2.00 in mint condition. A year later, with Seattle in the Finals, the value of his cards rose to $5.00. Similar increases were registered for Kemp's Skybox and Fleer rookie cards as well. The flock of memorabilia hounds that surrounds professional basketball knows that Shawn Kemp is a hot commodity. And he deserves the attention. His story is not just the tale of a great athlete; it is also the story of a young man who finally found himself. In the space of eight years, he went from being a raw 19-year-old rookie to one of the top players in the NBA.

Those who watch Kemp on the basketball court can sense the strength of his emotions.

Off-court he is quiet, thoughtful, and private, a man who cherishes good friends. In his free time in Seattle, Kemp volunteered for Read to Succeed, a youth literary project. At Christmas, he donned a Santa suit and distributed gifts to needy kids at community centers. But on the court, Kemp rages and stomps, showing friend and foe alike how much he cares and how hard he works.

Kemp's career in the NBA demonstrates how hard work and self-control can overcome bad breaks and give a player a chance to come through in the clutch. As a basketball player, Kemp followed the toughest road possible to the top but his inner drive and determination combined to make him a true legend of professional basketball.

CHRONOLOGY

1969   Shawn Travis Kemp is born in Elkhart, Indiana, on November 26.

1988   Shawn attends the University of Kentucky with his close friend, Chris Mills. The same year, he leaves Kentucky to attend Trinity Valley Community College in Texas to play with the TVCC Cardinals.

1989   On June 3 Shawn Kemp is selected by the Seattle SuperSonics as the 17th pick in the first round of the NBA draft.

1991   During a game against the Los Angeles Lakers on January 18 Shawn Kemp blocks ten shots, an all-time record for the Sonics.

1991   Shawn Kemp finishes second to Dee Brown in the slam-dunk competition during the All Star Weekend.

1994   Shawn scores a career-high 42 points against the Los Angeles Clippers on December 10.

1994   Shawn becomes a member of the gold medal-winning Dream Team II at the World Championships of Basketball in Toronto.

1996   Shawn Kemp's two successful free throws on June 2 win the seventh Western Conference game for the Sonics, enabling them to meet the Chicago Bulls in the NBA Finals.

1996   On June 16 the Chicago Bulls win the NBA Finals despite Shawn Kemp's personal best play.

1997   On September 25 Shawn Kemp is traded to the Cleveland Cavaliers in a three-way deal for Vin Baker.

STATISTICS

SHAWN KEMP

SEASON	TEAM	G	FGM	FGA	PCT	FTM	FTA	REB	PTS	PPG
89–90	SEA	81	203	424	.479	159	117	346	525	6.5
90–91	SEA	81	462	909	.508	288	436	679	1214	15.0
91–92	SEA	64	362	718	.504	270	361	665	994	15.5
92–93	SEA	78	515	1047	.492	358	503	833	1388	17.8
93–94	SEA	79	533	990	.538	364	491	851	1431	18.1
94–95	SEA	82	545	997	.547	438	585	893	1530	18.7
95–96	SEA	79	526	937	.561	493	664	904	1550	19.6
96–97	SEA	81	526	1032	.510	452	609	807	1516	18.7
Totals		625	3672	7054	.521	2822	3766	5978	10,148	16.2

PLAYOFF STATISTICS

SEASON	TEAM	G	FGM	FGA	PCT	FTM	FTA	REB	PTS	PPG
90–91	SEA	5	22	57	.386	22	27	36	66	13.2
91–92	SEA	9	48	101	.475	61	80	110	157	17.4
92–93	SEA	19	110	215	.512	93	15	190	313	16.5
93–94	SEA	5	26	70	.371	22	33	49	74	14.8
94–95	SEA	4	33	57	.579	32	39	48	99	24.8
95–96	SEA	20	147	258	.570	124	156	208	418	20.9
96–97	SEA	12	85	175	.486	87	105	148	259	21.6
Totals		74	471	933	.505	441	555	789	1386	18.7

G	games	PTS	points
FGM	field goals made	PPG	points per game
FGA	field goals attempted	FTA	free throws attempted
PCT	percentage	REB	rebounds
FTM	free throws made	AST	assists
FTA	free throws attempted	PTS	points
REB	rebounds	AVG	average

FURTHER READING

Hollander, Zander. 1996. *The Complete Handbook of Pro Basketball.* New York: Signet.

Moquin, Marc. 1996. *The 1997–97 Seattle Supersonics Media Guide.* Seattle Supersonics.

Naismith, James. 1996. *Basketball: Its Origin and Development.* Lincoln, NE: University of Nebraska Press.

Peterson, Robert. 1990. *Cages to Jumpshots: Pro Basketball's Early Years.* New York: Oxford University Press.

Sampson, Curt. 1995. *Full Court Pressure: A Tumultuous Season with Coach Karl & the Seattle Sonics.* New York: Doubleday.

ABOUT THE AUTHOR

Mike Bonner has written about sports for *Oregon Sports News*, *Sports Collector's Digest*, *Sports Card Gazette*, *Beckett Vintage*, and *Sports Map* magazine. From 1992 to 1993, Mike wrote a column about football cards for *Tuff Stuff* magazine.

In 1995, Mike's *Collecting Football Cards, A Complete Guide*, was published by Wallace Homestead Books of Radnor, Pennsylvania. A graduate of the University of Oregon, he is married to the former Carol Kleinheksel and has one daughter, Karen.

INDEX